THE ART
of
SAN SIMEON

Carol J. Everingham

Introduction to the Collection

Photography by Peter D'Aprix
Designed by Don French Graphic Design, Santa Barbara
Typography by Pickard Graphics, Santa Barbara

Collaboration on the text: Connie Rowley
Quotes: Eric Doyle
Notes on Plates: Alec Briones
Consultant on the Collection: Taylor Coffman

First Printing
Haagen Printing,
Santa Barbara, CA.

Printed in the United States of America

Dedicated to

the creative spirit of
William Randolph Hearst

and to

Architect *Julia Morgan*
who drew from it a reality

FOREWORD

I feel certain that Pop would have approved heartily of Carol Everingham doing this most essential work for many reasons.

One, no collection like his should have gone this long without a thorough documentation of all the works of art he collected. Her book is a splendid beginning.

Two, she has the academic background as her resumé confirms.

Lastly, she has a highly developed sense of enthusiasm; a characteristic which Pop much admired and sought after in writers and newspaper people in general.

I am pleased and honored that she asked me to write this little foreword as it gives me a good feeling to know that I had a hand in choosing her and in encouraging her.

She has captured the enchantment of the Enchanted Hill.

WILLIAM RANDOLPH HEARST, JR.
San Simeon, August 19, 1981

A great many fine things will be arriving for the ranch —
some of them have already arrived...

I had no idea when we began to build the ranch that
I would be here so much or that the construction itself
would be so important. Under the present circumstances,
I see no reason why the ranch should not be a museum of
the best things that I can secure...

William Randolph Hearst
to Julia Morgan
February 19, 1927

PLATE I: ROMAN SARCOPHAGUS c. 230 A.D. (COURT OF CASA DEL MONTE)

Come you then, let us begin from the Muses. . .
As they tell of what is, and what is to be,
and what was before now. . .
Hesiod, *Theogony*, 8th century B.C.

There were nine of them.
Epic poetry, lyric poetry, love poetry,
sacred song, dance, astronomy, drama,
history, and comedy were their attributes.
Zeus was their father, and Memory their mother.
Their leader was Apollo, his Radiant Light their inspiration.

The Muses.

Every four years, high on a mountaintop, they held a festival;
and their combined talents became the very soul of the Arts.
Their home was the Museum.

In the classical sense, *La Cuesta Encantada* is a Museum.
Art, music and science abound.
During the Twenties and Thirties, *The Enchanted Hill*
became a festival of the creative spirit — a gathering place
for scores of artisans and craftsmen who
carved, forged and molded dreams into reality.

In the modern sense, *La Cuesta Encantada* is the ultimate museum.
Not only do tapestries, rugs, sculpture, silver,
porcelain and paintings represent the Fine Arts,
but also, as Applied Arts, the very ceilings, doors, walls
and fireplaces incorporate vestiges of antiquity
which, in themselves, are artistic expressions
of the infinite creative drive of man.

Calliope, Euterpe, Erato, Polyhymnia, Terpsichore,
Urania, Melpomene, Clio and Thalia —
all the Muses are present
and their spirit still very much alive.

POTTERY
καλλιόπη epic poetry

Let the imagination run away. . .

    Join the sumptuous banquet table
        of Apollo, Athena, Hera and Zeus;
    attend a dust-raising chariot race
        as drivers compete for the Pythian prize;
    witness Greek and Trojan warriors
        in combat, clashing shields and spears;
    catch a glimpse of Nike, the winged victory,
        riding over the plains in her chariot;
    watch women spin wool in Ionic-columned houses
        or gather the fruit from abundant orchards;
    meet Ares, Achilles, Aphrodite —

Red figures on black, black figures on red, or geometric;
mythological events depicted on pottery. . .

Amphoria, hydria, krater, askos,
rhyton, kalpis, stamnos and pithos;
observe the sizes and shapes —
8th century to 1st century B.C.

Come, listen to the Muses
as they speak and sing of their Greeks
in epic proportions and picturesque detail.

But a skilled charioteer with slower horses, keeping his eye on the turning post, will cling to it as he takes the curve...

Homer, *The Iliad*, 8th century B.C.

PLATE II: GREEK AMPHORA. LATE GEOMETRIC, 8th c. B.C. (LIBRARY)

EARTHENWARE

In Italy, it's *maiolica*;
in France, it's *faïence*.

Earthenware's odyssey has been traced back
to ancient Assyria through fragments
from 8th century B.C. which show the use
of simple tin glazes on baked clay.

As colorful jugs and pots, earthenware
traveled the trade routes from central Asia
through the Islamic world to Medieval Spain
where Moorish artisans, inspired by Arab
and Islamic motifs, were prompted to use
glazes in a more decorative way.

As ornaments of beauty and value, reaching
15th century Italy via the island of *Majorca*,
earthenware became acknowledged
as a vehicle for artistic expression
when Renaissance artisans of Urbino and Faenza
painted portraits and classical themes
on stylized vases and plates.

Known as *Urbinoware* and *maiolica* of *Faenza*,
earthenware continued its odyssey into
16th century France where its production
attained prominence and became recognized
in Limoges as the art of *faïence*.

Now Pharoah's daughter went down to bathe in the river, and the girls attending her were walking along by the riverside. Among the reeds she noticed the basket. . .

Exodus 2:5

PLATE III: 17th c. ITALIAN MAJOLICA VASES, URBINO, ITALY (DOGES SITTING ROOM)

PORCELAIN/TILES

Dynasties of design and empires of color —
Chinese porcelain and Persian pottery
influenced each other due to trade routes.

Dappled T'ang glazes inspired Islamic imitations, while
Persian metallic pigments were simulated as Sung overglazes.
15th century "Ming blue" became 16th century "Kubachi blue"
as elaborate Chinese dragons turned into stylized Persian steeds.

Third century B.C. to 18th century A.D. —
China and Persia imitated each other,
as in the rug-like patterns of tiles from Kerman and Tabriz
resembling the delicate motifs of Chinese calligraphy.

And on it continues, the Persian-Chinese trade
of colors, form, and decoration
as evidenced in the spandrel
where yellow-jacketed warriors,
galloping forth on cobalt blue mounts,
oppose powder blue soldiers
astride bright yellow steeds;
and leaves on the trees reverse the patterns
of black and white chargers,
while curved-bladed sabers
follow contours of bending branches,
as two down-trodden horses lose their blueness
to the underworld underneath.

China and Persia, representing centuries of colors,
ideas and techniques, worked in customized reciprocity
leading to "*faïence*" in France and "maiolica" in Italy.

PLATE IV: 16th CENTURY PERSIAN TILE SPANDREL (BILLIARD ROOM)

If Persia's spoils invite thee to the field,
Accept the aid my conquering legions yield;
Led by two chiefs of valour and renown. . .

The march begins—the brazen drums resound,
His moving thousands hide the trembling ground;
For Persia's verdant land he wields his spear. . .

The Shāh-nāma, Abdul Ferdusi
10th c. Persia

CERAMICS

Well known in Florence for his reliefs in marble
and schooled in the delicate art of goldsmithing,
Luca di Simone di Marco della Robbia
was inspired by majolica as an exemplary method
of introducing color to sculpture.

The key to Luca's success was his devising
a tin glaze that lent the illusion of marble to terra cotta.
Together, Luca and his nephew, *Andrea*, made
bas reliefs and busts affordable to the people.

As the della Robbia fame spread, even into the palaces of France,
the secret of the tin glaze was passed on to Andrea's sons:
Luca II, a technician; *Ambrogio*, an artisan; *Mattia*, an artist;
Girolamo, the youngest, a painter, sculptor and architect; and
Giovanni, the eldest, whose spirit was most like that of his father.

All working in enameled terra cotta, yet in individual style,
they had produced, by the 1550's, a vast array of
adoring Madonnas, bas reliefs of St. Joseph and Child,
candleholders of angels, statues of St. Anthony of Padua,
busts of children, and the famed della Robbia wreaths
such as the tondo of glazed fruit and snails in their shells
which encircles a future Pope's coat-of-arms.

The secret of the glaze died with the last of the sons.
And the fragile mementos of this great Florentine family
frequently came to a sad end — such as the exquisite
della Robbias of the palace in Paris, destroyed during
the Revolution, and the colorful fragments being used
to mend French boulevards and avenues.

A façade of faïence, a triumph of polychromatic architecture. . .

rgio Vasari, *Lives of Most Eminent*
rs, *Sculptors, and Architects*, 1550.

PLATE V: ARMORIAL TONDO, GIOVANNI DELLA ROBBIA (CLOISTER 4)

SILVER
εὐτέρπη lyric poetry

Catherine the Great was Empress of Russia,
Frederick the Great, King of Prussia,
and Joseph II, Emperor of Austria,
while some little hammer in Munich
was gently tapping away.

Slowly a lion's head, garlands of leaves
and square scroll feet began to take shape.
Columns of silver, delicately sculptured,
formed contours stretching upward;
at the top were leaf cups
fashioned in a neo-classic style,
and soon the silver took on a new glow:

Candlesticks.

The last taps of the hammer
became the hallmark of the silversmith:
Peter Streissel, 1786, Munich.

PLATE VI: GERMAN SILVER CANDLESTICKS, 1786 (ASSEMBLY ROOM)

Silver, once a substance more precious
than gold, has been hammered,
throughout centuries and countries
into a multitude of shapes:

    silver candlesticks, silver sconces,
    silver plates, silver platters;
        a silver lamp with silver lace,
        a silver bust of Saint Ursula;
    a silver cup with sixteen shields,
    two Spanish silver mirrors;
        a silver banner
        with sunflowers and sheep
        on a nine-foot silver shaft;
    silver tankards with inscriptions,
    silver tazzas of Paradise;
        a silver Irish mace,
        a Russian silver cup;
    a silver beaker from the Guild of Potters,
    a silver Dutch windmill of the 1600's;
        a silver wine cistern
        inscribed with the arms
        of Sir Edward Hussey;
    silver baskets of silver fish
    on a silver saltcellar;
        a silver icon,
    a Spanish silver cross
    showing St. Matthew, St. Mark,
    St. Luke and St. John, c. 1500;
        and a gold-gilt silver plate
        embossed with the goddess Venus
        and Neptune, her father.

On Sunday, Saint Oswald's day, Antwerpe's artists invited all three of us to their Hall, where we partook of a lordly feast. . . and all the plates and dishes were silver and there were other exquisite ornaments. . . And when I was invited to take my seat, the whole company rose to their feet, as if in honor to a great man.

Albrecht Durer, *Diary*, 1520.

PLATE VII: NUREMBERG SILVER DISH, 1581 (GOTHIC STUDY)

BRASS/BRONZE/IRON

Armorer, smithy and consummate craftsman,
the peace-loving god Vulcan,
with workers he fashioned of gold,
forged shapeless metals into implements
for saber-rattling mortals.

The only lame and ugly god among the immortals,
he married Venus; and from this union
of the exquisite goddess of beauty
and the deformed god of the forge
was born the loveliness of craft in metal:

The gleam of brass —
    bowls and braziers, a 15th century Florentine dish,
    candlesticks and plaques, Nuremberg plates, and
    a lantern which illuminated some 16th century
    gondolier's passage on a dark Venetian night.

The antiquity of bronze —
    an Etruscan cista of the 3rd century A.D.
    and an early French mortar inscribed:
    "Paula Joseph Jorsetus, the maker,"
    and "Mese Naii, the restorer."

The ubiquity of iron —
    17th century Spanish candlesticks,
    16th century Italian plaques,
    15th century French mortars, Tuscan flag brackets,
    a Gothic anvil for forging suits of armor,
    plus a splendid array of andirons, including
    those in the shapes of Venus and Mars.

Mars is outstanding in strength among the planets, but Venus masters him...

Venus, when in conjunction with Mars, in opposition to him, or in reception, or watching from sextile or trine aspect, as we say, often checks his malignants... She seems to master and appease Mars, but Mars never masters Venus.

Commentary on Botticelli's "Venus and Mars" by Marsilio Ficino, 15th c. philosopher.

PLATE VIII: 16th c. ITALIAN BRONZE ANDIRONS (DOGES SUITE)

ORIENTAL RUGS

ερατώ love poetry

In weaving was entwined the lyricism of a lifestyle.
Woven into rugs were the philosophies of a people.
Nomads, villagers and city dwellers —
the art of living was the art of interweaving
lives of tradition, ideas and dreams into
visual patterns of self-expression.

Baktiari, Boukara, Cabistan, Kazak, Shiraz:
names of rugs — names of nomadic tribes.
Like the patterns on their rugs, they
zig-zagged and wandered from field to field.
Inherent in their weavings was a nomadic freshness
of unspoiled simplicity and robust charm.

Tent size determined rug size;
available roots and herbs decided color.
The warp, the weft, the nap, the fringe
were characteristically irregular in shape
yet consistent in design. Intrinsic beauty
of jagged landscapes and sinuous streams
assumed geometric form.
Colors were bold and restless:
distinctive deep reds of the *Boukara*,
ivory, blues and greens of the *Kazak*,
cobalt blue of the *Shiraz*,
and the *Baktiari*, ''The Lucky Ones''
grew a bit of cotton for
cotton warps to be crossed in
woolen wefts of yellow and green.

Tribes of tradition creating rugs
from lifetimes of patient wanderings
measured by handfuls of herbs
and shagginess of sheep.

My love pierces me like an arrow. I send flowers to my love and toast her with wine. She is beautiful as the flowers of the field and she intoxicates me. I cannot find her, my heart is broken. Your life will be easy if you believe in Allah.

Presented to the Just Prince of Ispahan. Ali Ak-bar the weaver. 1782.

Inscription in the Tabriz rug

PLATE IX: TABRIZ SILK RUG, 1782, PERSIA (NEW WING)

Tabriz, Meshed, Kerman:
cities and city dwellers —
These rugs, these people were
steeped in poetry, legend and myth.
They were cosmopolitan weavers
of rich historical heritage
producing rugs of exquisite color
and intricate detail.

The *Tabriz* —
creative weavers catering to passing caravans;
city poets weaving love poems
as merchandise for the marketplace;
rugs made of royal ''Tabriz blue''
with bazaar backgrounds, in palatial dimensions.
Polished creativity.

The *Meshed* —
civilized weavers conditioned by
centuries of crusaders
as Meshed was the ''Mecca''
of Persian pilgrimages;
their central medallions were
like stained glass in
cathedral reds and blues.
Commercial weavers tying knots
for prosperous pilgrims.

The *Kerman* —
cultural weavers creating motifs
which were inspired from the lives of
legendary figures and mythological heroes;
speechless beauty characterized by
quiet colors of ivory, rose,
light greens and blues.

Meanwhile Khosrow remained in the garden. . . In figure he is like a cypress and in feature like the Spring. He resembles a king in every respect, the garden from end to end is lit up by him. Clad in his breastplate he is like the flaming sun. From a branch hangs a golden shield and a slave with a girdle stands in service before him.

The Shāh-nāma, Abdul Ferdusi,
10th c. Persia

PLATE X: KERMAN MEDALLION RUG, C. 1890, PERSIA (ASSEMBLY ROOM)

Hamadan, Kurdistan, Turkestan:
rugs and regions —
Like the designs on their rugs,
the people of these areas were as varied
as they were related.
Farmers in summer, weavers in winter,
they tied knots by the light of crude-oil lamps
and in the heat of the hearth.
These are warm, vivid rugs
woven by plain and simple folk
for practical family use.
Oblong runners and scatter rugs
enhanced by camel's hair
were made to last generations.
Harmonious patterns
in rosette, paisley or almond-nut design
hold the vibrance
of rural beauty and local color —
folk art, as abundant and fertile
as the weaver's lot in life.

Whether they be rugs of
nomads, villagers or city dwellers,
the art of weaving incorporated
the aesthetics of a people.
Prayer rugs, palace rugs or
rugs for one's self, these
and a few from the provinces
of China, invite going over
with an understanding eye.

PAINTINGS

On the walls are pictured,
not landscapes and still lifes,
but painted portraits of:
Archduc Ferdinand of Austria
   by Christopher Amberger;
King Philip of Spain
   by Gonzales, court painter;
Emperor Trajan
   by Bernardo da Farenze;

Allessandro Allori's
Grand Duchess of Tuscany,
Bianca Capello,
   and
Alvisius Vandramin
   attributed to Tintoretto;

Napoléon Bonaparte is depicted
   by Jean-Léon Gérôme
Before the Sphinx and *In Cairo;*

by Franz Xavier Winterhalter:
Emperor Ferdinand-*Maximilian*-Joseph
   and
Empress Marie-*Charlotte*-Amélie
Augustine-Victoire-Léopoldine,
   known as ''Carlotta''

and the most prominent of all
in the large Gothic study,
William Randolph Hearst
   by his friend, Orrin Peck.

. . . in May you had already won my confidence and good will quite apart from all political considerations. I soon noticed that my little daughter also shared my views; it was therefore my duty to proceed with circumspection, and now we have the fine result that my daughter chooses this alliance and prefers it to all others that offer themselves and that I joyfully consent to her choice.

Acceptance of Marriage from King Leopold (Carlotta's father) to Archduc Franz Joseph (Maximilian's brother) October 31, 1856.

I find it quite incredible that the young Princess should be so much in advance of her (16) years in intelligence. . . she'll make a beauty when she gets older.

Maximilian, in a letter to his brother, Archduc Franz Joseph of Austria.

PLATE XI: EMPEROR MAXIMILIAN, 1864, WINTERHALTER (CASA DEL MAR)

I could not be happier than I am,
Max is perfection in every way.

Carlotta, in a letter to her father,
King Leopold of Belgium.

PLATE XII: EMPRESS CHARLOTTE, 1864, WINTERHALTER (CASA DEL MAR)

SACRED PAINTINGS
πολύμνια sacred song

Out of a dormant Medieval winter
into a blossoming Renaissance spring
stepped Italy.
Versed in classical Latin and Greek
yet contemplating in contemporary Italian,
the artists of Pisa, Siena and Florence
painted.
From the Umbrian hills of St. Francis of Assisi
came a new spirit of individuality;
from the frescoes of Padua and Parma,
a fresh inspiration.
The Black Death had run its course
and the court of the Medici was thriving.
Humanism had arrived.

Vanishing was the idealized nature
of the Madonna and Child.
No longer were painters
content with anonymity,
no longer were paintings
of pure Gothic line.
With palettes of prose
and brushes of realism,
the artists painted ethereal images
with tangible traits.

The "schools" of Siena, Pisa and Florence
were becoming "followers" of master artists
while the Madonna and Child were depicted
with books, pomegranates, and birds;
on balconies, in niches, with Alpine landscapes;
accompanied by saints and fair-haired angels
playing recorders and aeolian harps.

PLATE XIII: ENTHRONED MADONNA AND CHILD WITH SAINTS,
14th c. FLORENCE (NORTH GOTHIC)

*I give you this urgent advice, to make
an effort always to embellish with fine
gold and with good colors, especially
in the figure of Our Lady. . .*

The Craftsman's Handbook,
Cennino Cennini, 1308.

SCULPTURE/wood

The art of the cathedral was the art
of the 12th and 13th centuries.
In power were the Popes, and
the First Crusade had just ended.

Poitiers. . . St. Denis. . . Chartres. . . Paris
. . . Fossanova. . . Amiens. . . Salisbury. . .
Reims. . . Florence — one by one
great Gothic pinnacles pointed toward Heaven.
As cathedrals were constructed,
sculptors were commissioned to carve
statues of prophets and saints;
illuminated manuscripts furnished the subjects
and Gothic dimensions provided the space.

Wood was a model medium,
unlike stone which came in blocks,
wood was naturally tall and narrow
in perfect Gothic proportion.

Statues in wood — 13th through 16th centuries:
a Flemish archbishop, a French St. Martin,
Venetian angels, a Spanish St. John,
A Tyrolian St. Barbara with tower and book,
and, garbed in a cloak of polychromed gold,
a Byzantine St. Peter as Pope.

Busts of wood
were carved to hold relics of saints
as cathedrals became pilgrimage points.
Reliquary busts, gilded and polychromed,
displayed their sacred treasure
for pilgrims, priests, and Popes.

We know not whether we were in Heaven or on Earth, for surely there is no such splendor or beauty anywhere upon Earth. . .

Envoys of Vladimir, Prince of Kiev, after seeing St. Sophia's in Constantinople

PLATE XIV: ST. PETER AS POPE, 13th c., SPAIN (GOTHIC SUITE)

SCULPTURE/bronze

The bronze rage began in 1401
with the Baptistry doors. A competition
for sculptors was held in Florence
to depict "The Sacrifice of Isaac"
in twenty bronze panels.

In 1430, an inspired Donatello created *David*,
the first lifesize bronze since antiquity;
and by the 1500's, freed from the constraints
of cathedral architecture, sculptors were
designing pieces for private gardens and palaces.

Bronzes ranging from busts of Roman
emperors to statuettes of river gods
adorned mantels, fountains and tables.
By sunlight or by candlelight, the lustre
and patina of bronze had a captivating effect.

In 1617, Giovanni Lorenzo Bernini, at the age of 19,
captured the desperate chase of Apollo and Daphne
with such élan that he was invited to the court of Louis XIV.
Encouraged by the Sun King to carve in grandiose style,
from elaborate fountains to ornate tombs,
Bernini chiseled Baroque curves which led
to Rococo swirls, and inspired succeeding generations
of sculpture in bronze such as Fremiet's "Minerva"
and Wieneman's "Descending Night."

Bronze replicas of the great marbles were cast
to lend a classical aura to the garden ambiance
and to evoke the past in the privacy of one's palace.

But Cardinal Borghese, to whom it seemed that it was by chance—as indeed it was—that he had discovered a treasure in this great creator, would not permit him to remain in his service without some beautiful work underway, so he had him (Bernini) carve the group of the youthful Apollo with Daphne who is in the process of changing into a laurel tree. . . In its design, in the proportions, in the expression of the heads, in the exquisiteness of all the parts, and in the fineness of its workmanship it surpasses anything imaginable. . . I need only say that as soon as it was finished such acclamation arose that all Rome rushed to view it as though it were a miracle.

The Life of Bernini,
Filippo Baldinucci, 1682.

PLATE XV: APOLLO AND DAPHNE, BERNINI, c. 1617 (DOGES SUITE)

SCULPTURE/stone
τερψιχόρη. dance

From an imperturbable ''Sekhmet''
sitting on her throne of 3500 years
to a sensuous ''Galatea''
borne on the back of a dolphin,
the dynamics of sculpture are
choreographed out of inert masses of stone.

Whether it be ''Venus Rising from the Sea''
or ''Venus Triumphant'' holding the apple of victory,
the emotional impact of a free-standing figure
communicates a feeling of vitality.

The spirit of the stonecarver
parallels that of the choreographer.
Axis, balance and inflection
are common denominators.
Posture, gesture and overall design make
MacMonnie's ''Enchanté'' an alluring solo,
Gérôme's ''Pygmalion and Galatea'' a pas de deux.

Taken into consideration are
the effects of light and shade.
From dazzling dawn to positioned spotlight,
a continuity of expression is reflected
by a three-dimensional figure in space.

Sculpture in stone abounds on the Hill,
dancing silently in the mind of the beholder;
an *esprit de corps* Egyptian to modern
with backgrounds of tapestries or
reflecting in pools of spring water.

O whitest Galatea, can it be
That thou shouldst spurn me off
who love thee so?

Come up, O Galatea, from the ocean,
And, having come, forget again to go!

Theocritis, Greek poet, 3rd c. B.C.
Translated by Elizabeth Barrett Browning

PLATE XVI: "GALATEA" ATTRIBUTED TO ANSIGLIONI, c. 1882 (MAIN TERRACE)

ARCHITECTURAL MOTIFS
οὐρανία astronomy

*I have thought a great deal over whether to make
this whole group of buildings Baroc (sic), in
the Eighteenth Century style, or Renaissance.
It is quite a problem. I started out with the
Baroc idea in mind, as nearly all the Spanish
architecture in America is of that character. . .
The alternative is to build this group of buildings
in the Renaissance style of Southern Spain. . .
The Renaissance of Northern Spain seems to me very
hard, while the Renaissance of Southern Spain is
much softer and more graceful. . . I would very much
like to have your views on what we should do. . .*

WRH to JM, Dec. 31st

The year is 1919.
William Randolph Hearst is 56
and his architect, Julia Morgan, 47.

In a collaboration that will continue
for another thirty years,
Hearst, the Medieval romantic,
and Morgan, the Beaux-Arts scholar,
will fashion his dream
out of tons of concrete and steel.

Incorporated into the structure
will be hundreds of architectural motifs
such as columns, doors, arches,
window frames, mantels, and ceilings,
from Medieval, Gothic and Renaissance Europe.

PLATE XVII: EARLY 18th c. ITALIAN COFFERED CEILING (DOGES SUITE)

*Under the circumstances I had probably best tell you
a little more of what he (Mr. Hearst) is doing here.
So far we have received from him to incorporate in the
new buildings, some twelve or thirteen carloads of
antiques, brought from the ends of the earth and from
prehistoric down to late Empire in period, the majority,
however, being of Spanish origin. . . I don't see myself
where we are ever going to use half suitably, but I
find that the idea is to try things out and if they are
not satisfactory, discard them for the next thing that
comes that promises better. There is interest and
charm coming gradually into play.*

Morgan to Byne, Nov. 18, 1921

Like putting together an immense
three-dimensional puzzle, the key to
incorporating antique parts into
a concete framework was in
finding the piece that fit.

As master sleuths, Hearst in New York,
Morgan in San Francisco, and Byne in Madrid,
ferreted out fragments of Spanish antiquity.
Documented by fourteen years of
correspondence, their story is
steeped in adventure and suspense.

From initial drawing to built-in reality
they assembled, element by element,
motif by motif, the enchanting character
and personality of San Simeon.

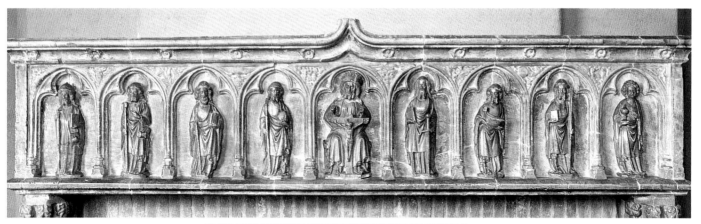

PLATE XVIII: ENGLISH GOTHIC FIREMANTEL (CLOISTER 1)

. . . and othere bookes of legendes of seintes, and omelies, and moralitee, and devocioun, that thanke I oure Lord Jhesu Crist and his blisful Mooder, and alle the seintes of hevene, bisekynge hem that they from hennes forth unto my lyves ende sende me grace to biwayle my giltes, and to studie the salvacioun of my soule, and graunte me grace of verray penitence, confessioun and satisfaccioun to doon in this present lyf, thrugh the benigne grace of hym that is kyng of kynges and preest over all preestes, that boghte us with the precious blood of his herte; so that I may been oon of hem at the day of doom that shulle be saved.

Heere is ended the book of the tales of Caunterbury, compiled by Geffrey Chaucer, of whos soule Jhesu Crist have mercy. Amen. 1394.

FURNITURE
μελπομένη drama

As objects which tend to increase
comfort through design and mobility,
furniture also sets the scene and defines the mood.

Scene I. 16th century France,
      a *hôtel particulier* in the province of Burgundy.

Early morning. Silence.
The soft light of dawn breaks the darkness.
Vertical lines of linenfold patterns
on the chasublier, armoires and
baldaquin bed are faintly visible.
In the sitting room, silhouettes of tiny
gargoyles and gilded pinnacles on the
flamboyant chest flicker in the glow
of the hearth's dying embers. In the study,
allegorical figures of tapestry-covered
chairs come to life as the gentle daylight
filters through rose-glazed windows.
Footsteps can be heard. . .

Scene II. 17th century Italy,
      a *palazzo* on the outskirts of Florence.

High noon. Sunshine is streaming in.
The air is hot and humid. Highlighted by the
brilliant rays is the patina of an octagonal
table with lion claw feet In the central
room, a baron's crowned escutcheon is outlined
on the finely carved cassone.

*Have pity on this armchair, it has been
stretching out its arms to you for a
quarter of an hour. . .*
Molière (1622-1673),
French playwright.

PLATE XIX: FRENCH RENAISSANCE ARMCHAIR (GOTHIC STUDY)

Against the walls of the study,
two Florentine credenzas
are immediately discernable, while a rare
eighteen-sided table is obscured by a
massive palace table which dominates the room.
Near the back wall, the works of Machiavelli
rest on an unusual triangular lectern.
A messenger arrives with the news. . .

Scene III. 18th century Spain,
         a *hacienda* in Catalonia.

Early evening. The sun is setting.
An arid breeze wafts through an open window.
To the right, a vargueño with inlaid bone panels
and gilded drawers rests on a baluster stand.
To the left, griffins on a
small Mudejar coffer seem to dance in
the last rays of the setting sun, while
slanted legs of a Moorish table project
elongated shadows on the rug. In the sitting
room, piñowood chairs have been pushed aside
to display the recently acquired arcón,
the marriage chest, its open gilded cover
gleaming in the waning light. From the patio
congenial sounds of laughter fill the evening sky. . .

The stage is set. Furnished are the scenes;
not three, but one —
the Gothic Suite and Study.

PLATE XX: SPANISH MARRIAGE CHEST, 15th c. (LOWER SOUTH DUPLEX)

TAPESTRIES
κλειώ history

Tapestries and newspapers — interwoven tabloids
unfolding before the spectator's very eyes,
were meant to be examined in full detail.
The art of tapestry was the art of reportage
where incidents from the lives of particular
people were given perspective and scope.

"SCIPIO RECEIVES CARTHAGINIAN OFFICERS"

"BATTLE OF THE TECINO"

"THE TRIUMPH OF RELIGION"   "THE ENCOUNTER"

Tapestries were like front pages —
their titles like banner headlines.
They told stories, depicted events.
Battle scenes, miracles, heroic deeds
became visual substances of the material image.
Time was captured on a two-dimensional surface.

Weavers and journalists — chroniclers
spinning together threads,
inch by inch, column by column
as creative communiqués passed on to posterity.

PLATE XXI: "RENCONTRE" (THE ENCOUNTER), BRUSSELS, 1696 (REFECTORY BALCONY)

The "Daniel" tapestries were among the
favorites of William Randolph Hearst:

> *These are most special. They were woven when the beauty of creative work was understood by the workmen who executed it as well as the artist who designed it and by the man who was willing to pay them both for the time to do it.*

> *Catherine de Medici was the great-granddaughter of Lorenzo the Magnificent, these were begun the day she was born as part of her hope chest; she took them when she went to wed the son of the King of France in 1553.*

These tapestries not only illustrated biblical verse, but,
as Mr. Hearst is quoted by Adela Rogers St. John in *The Honeycomb*,
in tapestries were also spun their own tales —
new yarns passed on for future generations to unravel...

> *Exactly as we are looking at them now, so did little Mary Stuart, Scotland's princess who had married the King of France... stand fascinated by them, as children now are by fairy tales, until she heard behind her the Old Queen's footsteps...*

PLATE XXII: "DANIEL" TAPESTRY, EARLY 16th c. FLEMISH (REFECTORY)

Everything rejoiced at the Spring. . .
From the herbs arose a sweet smell
Which the clear air made sweeter still,
And winding through the valley
A little brook passed
Moistening the lands
Of which the water was fresh.
There drank the little birds
After they had fed upon crickets,
Little flies and butterflies.
I saw there falcons and hawks
And beautifully plumed merlins,
And flies with a sting, and bees
Who bake pavilions of fine honey
In quantities by the trees.
In another part was the embrace
Of a charming meadow, where nature
Had strewn flowers on the verdure
White, yellow, red, and violet.

Alain Chartier, 15th c. Flemish

The minutes of the hour,
the months of the year —
daily life was depicted,
not in heroic flashes
but as visions of pastoral charm.

From large Flemish looms
emerged descriptive tableaux —
landscapes rather than legends
composed in woolen threads.

Tapestries and journals —
diaries of common folk
revealing what the day was like
and how the minutes were spent.

PLATE XXIII: "LABORS OF THE MONTHS," 17th c. FLEMISH (MORNING ROOM)

TEXTILES

Textiles play more than merely decorative parts,
velvet, silk, damask, linen and rare lace
have, in various fashions or forms, more practical roles.

Rose damask rather than panelling —

> *As a matter of fact, I think this damask*
> *which is about the shade of the sofas,*
> *will be so good looking in the room that*
> *we will not want anything else there.*
> *So we need not make the panelling at all.*
>
> WRH to JM, May 8, 1928

Red velvet instead of tapestries —

> *Tapestries would be rather ineffective on the walls*
> *unless we had a series of tapestries. . . the alternative*
> *is to use Byne's velvet over asbestos board. . . the*
> *Theatre must be practicable from an acoustic point of*
> *view, and I do not see why it cannot be beautiful too.*
>
> WRH to JM, February 26, 1930

Functional beauty —
fifteenth-century chasubles and seventeenth-century copes
hang on walls like finely woven pictures; vestments of
priests and banners of popes lend an air of serenity.

Most striking, perhaps, are the festive silk flags,
processional banners of 16th century Siena, which wave
like supple panes of stained glass before Gothic windows.

Expressions of beauty, visual and tactile —
the quintessence of textiles.

*On the sea coast there is a city. . . its port is
frequented by merchants from Venice. . . the
country produces a great quantity of silk, and a
manufacture is carried on of silks (of crimson)
interwoven with gold.*

Travels of Marco Polo, The Venetian, 14th c.

FANTASIES
Θάλεια comedy

Fantasies — The perfect union of subject, material and
technique in which design and craftsmanship
are more important than precious substances:

rose quartz, carved in the shape of immortal Ho-Sien Ku,
serves as the standard for a beautiful lamp;
ivory, sculptured in a series of hunting scenes,
becomes an exotic 17th century goblet;
rock crystal, ebony, gilded bronze,
lapis lazuli and filigreed gold
create a jewel coffer — fit for a king.

Fantasies —Works of imagination and charm, often made
from simple and inexpensive materials:

the horn of a buffalo
is transformed into a drinking cup
which rests on golden griffin feet;
paper, bound with moroccan leather in 1846,
forms a book whose gilt fore-edge,
when spread obliquely, reveals a lovely
miniature of ''Evenings at Hadden Hall'';
glass, blown and frosted, by René Lalique,
emerges as a bowl with doves
eternally perched on its rim.

Fantasies —Exquisite pieces designed to engage the spirit
and delight the eye as flights of fancy
in tangible form — the captivating products
of ingenious artisans and their musings.

Why should we not drink, when our country, sitting on dry land, is drinking too. Drinking seals the bond of friendship.

The Rain, Harsdorffer,
15 c. German poet

PLATE XXV: "GRIFFINCLAW" 15th c. GERMAN DRINKING HORN (GOTHIC STUDY)

That Feast of Peaches Immortal. . . is now surpassed by this Banquet for Peace in Heaven. Dragon flags and phoenix chariots stand glowing in halos bright, as standards and blazing banners whirl in hallowed light. Sweet are the tunes of immortal airs and songs. . .

Peach Blossom Spring, T'ao Ch'ien, 4th c. A.D.

PLATE XXVI: ROSE QUARTZ FIGURE OF HO-SIEN KU, CH'ING DYNASTY (NORTH GOTHIC)

ACKNOWLEDGEMENTS begin with *Richard Avedon* who first shared in my visions of creating a book on the art of San Simeon and encouraged me to meet and present my ideas to *William Randolph Hearst, Jr.* in New York. Expressing his support for an art book series, Mr. Hearst provided the initial momentum towards its realization. A grant from *The Hearst Foundation* to *The California State Parks Foundation* launched the project in February 1981.

Enthusiastic support was offered by *Dr. Dale Andrews, David Walch* and *Bob Blesse* of California Polytechnic State University at San Luis Obispo, who, with the assistance of *Dottie Stechman*, permitted me to research and quote from the newly-bestowed gift of the Julia Morgan-William Randolph Hearst Correspondence. Many hours were also spent with *Virginia Crook* at the San Luis County Library.

Sara Holmes Boutelle was instrumental in sharing her thoughts on the concept of art in architecture and her extensive knowledge of Julia Morgan. *Ann Miller* provided invaluable assistance in the documentation of art objects; *Melody Brazzil* was most generous in communicating her love of fabrics and textiles; *Woody Yost* lent insight into the Oriental Rug and Greek Pottery Collections. A special thanks to *Nancy Martin* for her energy during long hours of late night photography, to *Alice McIntyre* in New York for her editorial insights into the manuscript, and to *Albert Field* for his technical printing advice.

A very warm "thank you" to *Freedom Barry* and *Audrey Galli* whose perception into the poetry and charm of the Enchanted Hill has kept me continually inspired. Sincere thanks to *Caroline Boniface* and *Metta Hake* for their understanding and support.

Much appreciation and credit to the entire staff at the Hearst-San Simeon State Historical Monument and especially: *Gerry Fialho, Dan Goswick, Irene Horne, Phyllis Aitken, Thelma Anderson, Sue Archer, Jim Ballinger, Liz Barnes, Zell Bordegaray, George Butterfield, Morris Cecil, Jerry Chaffin, Art Chandler, Dorothy Collins, Ardis Cousins, Rick Cress, Betty de Lancellotti, Charles de Vogel, The Doyles, Merry Ellis, Toni Evans, Jim Fajardo, Shannon Harmon, Janet Horton-Payne, Leah Ireland, Daisy Johnson, Dennis Judd, Vickie Kastner, Virginia Kecker, Bob Kruyer, Bob Latson, David Locke, Patty Lockett, Carolyn Martin, Joyce McDevitt, John Melvin, Terizza Miller, Dave Norby, Joe & Rita Nunes, Grayson Orr, Debbie Palmer, Aline Paul, John Porter, Donna Pultz, Gail Ridley, Tom Scott, Arles Tooker, Ron & Denise Whaley, Betty Whitman, Al Wilhelm* and *Jim Woodruff.*

Very welcomed were the contributions of *Mary Baldwin, Tara Blackburn, Stefan & Francie Kozinski, Millie Lawless* and *Jack Smith*. My deep gratitude to *Michel Butor, Mrs. W.R. Hearst, Jr., Mel London* and *Mr. & Mrs. R.I.E. Jr. & Sr.*

C.J.E.

PLATES

Note: Objects in the Hearst-San Simeon Collection are identified by a PC (Pacific Coast Register) and/or a corresponding HE (Hearst Estate) number.

Plate I. Marble Sarcophagus, c. 230 A.D., believed to be from Palazzo Barberini, Rome. Elaborate high relief figures on front panel (L. to R.) of the Muses: Polyhymnia (Sacred Song) holding scroll; Terpsichore (Dance) holding two pipes; Thalia (Comedy) with mask and pipe; Melpomene (Drama) carrying a mask and the club of Hercules; Euterpe (Lyric Poetry) with lyre and plectrum; Apollo, leader of the Muses, holding Python serpent staff; Athena, Goddess of Wisdom and the Arts, in full armor with helmet, a griffin at her feet; Clio (History) with scroll; Erato (Love Poetry) holding a small lyre; Urania (Astronomy) shown with celestial globe and stiletto; and Calliope (Epic Poetry) with tablet and stylus. H. 2'10'' L. 7'6'' W. 2'8'' PC 6256. Acquired at the Charles T. Yerkes Sale, American Art Association, New York, April 11-13, 1910, No. 255.

Plate II. Greek Amphora, Late Geometric, c. 740 B.C. Referred to as the ''Baring Amphora'' from the Lord Revelstoke (né Cecil Baring) Collection. First published in *Antiquarian Quarterly*, Vol. 1, 1925-26; later by Bell in *California Studies in Classical Antiquity*, Vol. 4, pp. 81-91, plates 1-5. H. 23'' PC 7641/HE 5559. Acquired at the Lord Revelstoke Sale, Puttick & Simpson, London, April 5, 1935, No. 9.

Plate III. Pair Majolica Vases, late 16th century, Urbino, Italy. Tin-glazed earthenware with intricate pictorial narratives, back of each with central figure wearing a crown, at the bases the inscription: FATTO IN VRBINO. H. 22'' PC 8758/HE 6185. Acquired from Spanish Art Gallery, Ltd., London, July 15, 1932.

Plate IV. Persian Tile Spandrel, 16th century, from the Palace Tchihil Sutun, near Ispahan. Scenes on the 34 enameled tiles were inspired by the *Shāh-nāma* of Ferdusi. H. 4'6'' L. 8'8'' PC 3043. Acquired at the H. Kevorkian Sale, Anderson Galleries, New York, March 16-18, 1922, No. 579.

Plate V. Armorial Tondo by Giovanni della Robbia (1469-1529), Florence. Escutcheon believed to be that of the prelate Giovanni Maria del Monte (Pope Julius III). Dia. 27'' PC 3416. Acquired at the Raoul Tolentino Sale, American Art Association, New York, December 8-11, 1926, No. 718.

Plate VI. Pair of Silver Candlesticks, bearing the hallmarks: Peter Steissel, Munich, 1786. H. 34'' PC 895/HE 6286. Acquired from Arnold Seligmann, Rey & Co., New York, May 16, 1934.

Plate VII. Silver-gilt Dish, Nuremberg, dated: 1581; maker's mark: B.I. Boldly embossed rim, and center medallion of Neptune and Venus. Dia. 17'' PC 10586/HE 5387. Acquired from Sotheby & Co., London, 1937.

Plate VIII. Pair of Venetian Andirons, 16th century, figures of Venus and Mars in bronze. H. 31'' PC 3046/HE 6204. Acquired from Bacri Frères, Paris, 1928.

Plate IX. Royal Persian Silk Carpet, Tabriz, dated 1782. Entire field with cartouches of Farsi love poems. L. 12'5'' W. 9'5'' PC 1744/HE 6681. Acquired at the Mrs. William A. Morgan Sale, American Art Association-Anderson Galleries, New York, February 23-25, 1933, No. 564.

Plate X. Persian Medallion Rug, Kerman c. 1890. Figures believed to be from the *Shāh-nāma* (*Book of Kings*), depicting the romance of Khosrow Parviz and Shirin, by Persia's greatest epic poet, Abul Qasem Ferdusi (c. 940-1020 A.D.). Border inscription: I AM A FOLLOWER OF AL-HASAIN. L. 22'2'' W. 14'3'' HE 6291. Provenance unknown.

Plate XI & XII. Portraits of Emperor Maximilian and Empress Charlotte of Mexico. Signed and dated: Winterhalter, Paris, 1864. Oil on canvas. H. 39½'' W. 29½'' PC 9188/HE 4643. Acquired from Goldschmidt Galleries, London, 1937.

Plate XIII. Enthroned Madonna and Child with Saints, c. 1410. Painted figures on wood of the Holy Mother as Queen of Heaven, holding the Infant Savior, and flanked by Saints John, Mark, Francis,, Luccia, Margaret, and Catherine (their names inscribed in their halos). Once attributed to the School of Pisa, is now believed to be the work of Jacopo da Firenze. H. 50'' W. 22½'' PC 880/HE 5123. Acquired at the Achillito Chiesa Sale Part IV, American Art Association, New York, November 22-23, 1927, No. 70.

Plate XIV. Statue of Saint Peter as Pope, 13th century, Spanish, in Byzantine style. Polychromed wood. Peter, the first Pope, is wearing the conical papal tiara; in his left hand, he is holding a Bible, in his right hand, he once held a crosier. H. 42½'' PC 3392/HE 5212. Acquired at the Conde de las Almenas Sale, American Art Association, New York, January 13-15, 1927, No. 109.

Plate XV. Apollo and Daphne. Attributed to Giovanni Lorenzo Bernini (1598-1680). Thought to be a studio bronze model for the lifesize marble in the Borghese Palace, Rome. Depicts the climactic moment of Daphne's transformation into a laurel tree. H. 2'11'' PC 2733/HE 6189. Acquired from J. & S. Goldschmidt, Frankfurt, December 9, 1931.

Plate XVI. Galatea. Attributed to Leopoldo Ansiglioni, Rome, c. 1882, marble. An identical version of Galatea reclining on the back of a dolphin, with curling waves below her feet, is located at the Lillie Langtry Estate, London, and is signed by Ansiglioni. (cf. *Avery Hill Winter Garden*, a Greater London Publication). H. 6' L. 4'6'' PC 9838. Provenance unknown.

Plate XVII. Detail of Italian Coffered Ceiling, early 18th century. Carved walnut with painted panels and beams, once possibly a larger unit, the ceiling appears to have been divided for two rooms. PC 5141. Acquired from French & Co., New York, April 2, 1924.

Plate XVIII. English Gothic Mantel, sculptured alabaster. High relief figures of saints and their attributes, and a central figure of the Father holding a crucifix. H. 17¼'' L. 6'7½'' PC 5374. Acquired from Charles of London, New York, July 31, 1923.

Plate XIX. French Renaissance Armchair. One in a set of twelve with backs and seats covered in allegorical tapestries. H. 48'' W. 20½'' D. 24'' PC 6388-89/HE 5374. Acquired at the Luigi Orselli Sale, American Art Association, New York, February 15-19, 1921, Nos. 823-24 (two lots of six).

Plate XX. Arcón (Spanish Marriage Chest), 15th century, Catalonian. Polychromed and gilded walnut. Painting inside the lid depicts Saint Peter meeting Christ on the road, with the inscription: DO THAT WHICH YOU PROMISED ME IN AS MUCH AS I FOR YOUR SAKE DID THAT WHICH I PROMISED YOU. H. 26½'' L. 49½'' D. 22½'' PC 3481/HE 6056. Acquired at the Francis Wilson Mark Sale, Anderson Galleries, New York, February 10-12, 1927, No. 528.

Plate XXI. Rencontre (The Encounter) Tapestry, c. 1696, Brussels. Believed to be part of the eight-piece Marlborough Set entitled *The Art of War*, designed by Lamert de Honte. Signed: A. CASTRO (pseudonym of the weaver, Gaspard van der Borch), town mark: BB (Brabant Brussels). Wool and silk. Often called the ''Munich Set,'' seven other panels depicting military life, are:

Campement, Fachinade, Embuscade, Pillage, La Marche, Fouragement, and Attaque. H. 13'2'' L. 16'5'' PC 9280/HE 6326. Exhibited at the Palace of Fine Arts, San Francisco, in 1917. From the Phoebe A. Hearst Collection.

Plate XXII. Gothic Tapestry, early 16th century, Flemish. One of two silk and wool tapestries showing the prophet Daniel amidst a crowd of nearly 50 figures as he interprets the dreams of King Nebuchadnezzar, with Arioch, the head executioner, standing nearby. Names of the three principals are woven into their robes. H. 11'5'' L. 21'4'' PC 6678-79/HE 6327. Acquired from Arnold Seligmann, Rey & Co., New York, March 28, 1923.

Plate XXIII. Flemish Tapestry, 17th century, Brussels. Wool and silk. One of four from a set entitled *Labors of the Months*, this particular one illustrating the month of May. Pastoral scenes represented by the other three are: July (hay harvest), August (corn harvest) and October (grape harvest). The existence of other months is unknown, but a similar July panel is located at the Bowes Museum, Durham County, England. H. 10' L. 11'9'' PC 6672-75/HE 6379. Provenance unknown.

Plate XXIV. Venetian Cope, 15th century Gothic, with hood and orphrey designs of saints attributed to Francesco Squarcione (1391-1474). Gold needle-painted velvet. H. 4'6'' L. 9'10'' PC 9962/HE 4580. Acquired from the James A. Garland Sale, American Art Association, New York, January 17-19, 1924, No. 428.

Plate XXV. ''Griffinclaw'' Drinking Horn, 15th century Gothic, German or Upper Italian. Buffalo horn with copper-gilt mounting on two claw feet. H. 8'' Dia. 3¾'' PC 2925/HE 5345. Acquired at the Fritz August von Kaulbauch Sale, Hugo Helbing, Munich, October 29-30, 1929.

Plate XXVI. Carved Rose Quartz Statuette, fitted as a lamp, Chinese, Ch'ing Dynasty (1644-1912). Figure of Ho-Sien Ku, the daughter of a humble shopkeeper, who ate the peach of immortality given to her by Shou-sing, God of Longevity. Living in 7th century A.D., the only woman among the eight immortals, she decreed that reverence be paid with a special flower for each month. Her wishes became the Chinese flower calendar. H. 27'' PC 2362/HE 5119. Acquired at the William Cowan Sale, American Art Association-Anderson Galleries, New York, October 20-24, 1931, No. 499.

Born fifth generation on the Everingham dairy farm in upstate New York, Carol has been traveling since her graduation from high school. Combining four years of French studies with "on location" exploration of art and literature, Ms. Everingham spent a year at the University of Bordeaux while discovering 94 of the 95 départements. Two years of Master studies at Nice, under the tutelage of author Michel Butor, incorporated her reading of *A la Recherche du Temps Perdu* (Remembrance of Things Past) by Marcel Proust with travels to its numerous literary settings in France and Italy. This research culminated in a thesis on the color *Mauve Chez Proust* which obtained highest French honors from the University of Nice in 1972. Doctoral studies in Paris, at the Sorbonne and the Louvre, pursuing the theme of Salomé in art, music and literature, led to a journey throughout Europe and the Middle East where she spent a summer in Israel on Kibbutz En-Dor. A final odyssey before returning to the United States was designed to explore the myth of Apollo at various sites in Greece.

A certified French teacher, Ms. Everingham has taught at Scarsdale Central School and was the cross-cultural coordinator and teacher of a French immersion program at the Purnell School in New Jersey. She has been on the staffs of the Lycée Français de New-York and the United Nations in bilingual capacities. At the Museum of Modern Art in New York she was an assistant to the Director of Drawings, William S. Lieberman; and at the University Art Museum in Berkeley, floor manager of the Richard Avedon Retrospective.

A visit to the Hearst State Historical Monument in 1980 so enraptured her that, upon discovering there were no books on the Collection, she set forth to produce an art book designed not only to describe the scope and uniqueness of the art and architecture by category, but also to convey the vitality and warmth with which W.R. Hearst and Julia Morgan created the Enchanted Hill.